How the model hovercraft works

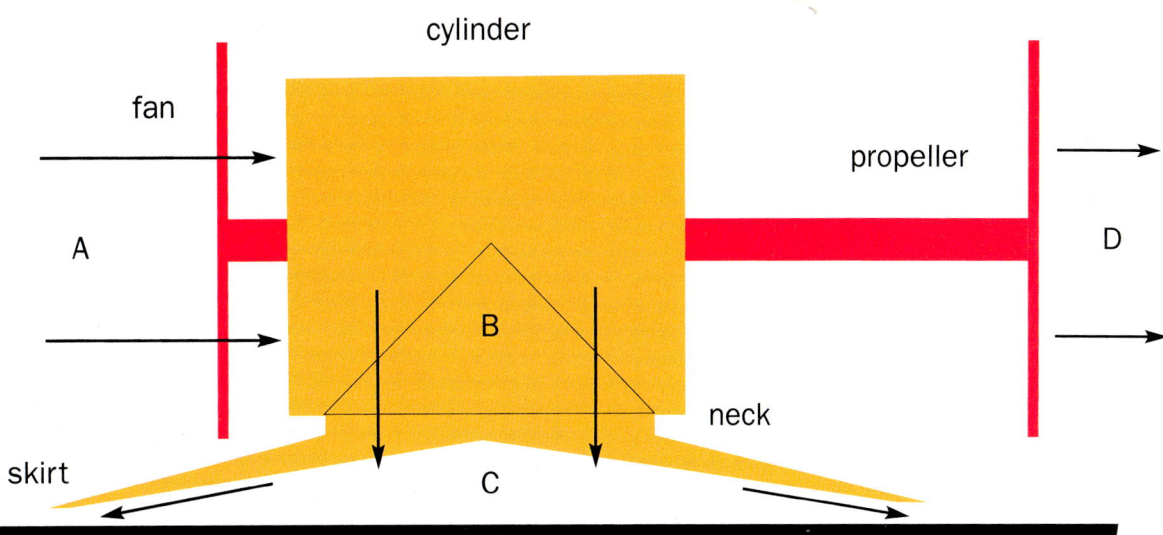

A - The fan compresses air into the cylinder

B - Air is forced down the neck into the space under the skirt

C - Air escapes round the rim of the skirt, lifting the hovercraft up

D - The propeller pushes the hovercraft forward as it floats on the cushion of air beneath the skirt.

Contents

Step 1

Cut out the seven red segments which make up the lower skirt (pages 15, 17, 35 & 43) and lay them on a flat work surface using polythene sheet to protect it from stray glue. Glue the segments together by putting glue on the white tab and laying the next segment on top of the tab. Make sure the coloured part of one segment covers the white tab of the next segment exactly with no overlap. Don't glue the final tab yet.

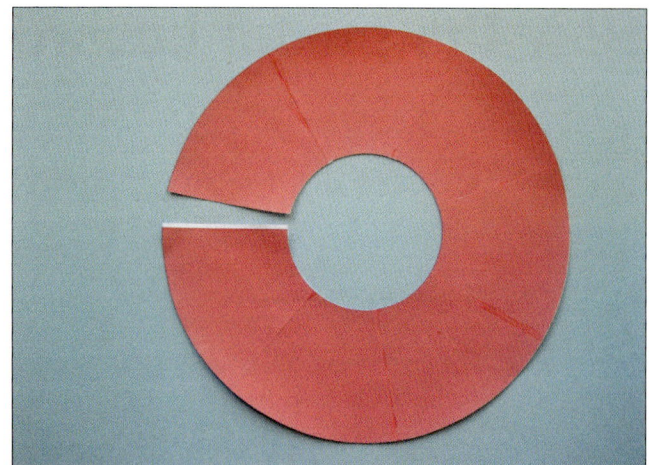

Step 2

Cut out the Lower Skirt Gap Template (page 33). The template is not part of the model - it is used to ensure that the gap in the ring is exactly the right size.

Lay the template so that it exactly covers the remaining white tab, bridges the gap, and rests on the opposite segment. Then draw a pencil line along the stencil's edge.

Finally cut the tab along the pencil line.

Step 3

Put glue on the remaining white tab and join the lower skirt up.

Turn the skirt upside down and lay it down on the table.

Leave it to dry for 20 minutes or so during which time it should settle into its conical shape.

When the glue is dry, turn the skirt over so the red side is upwards

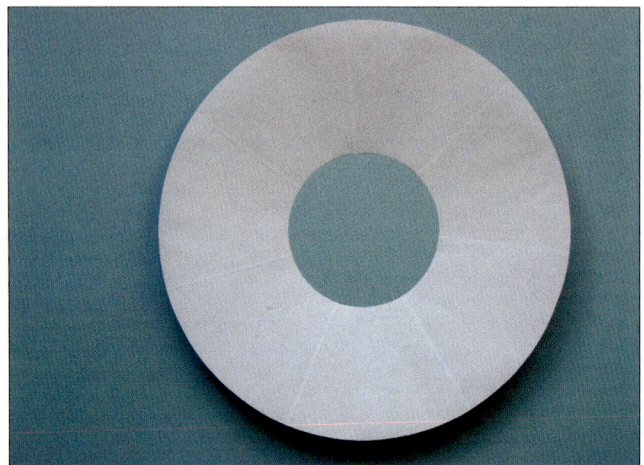

Step 4

Cut out the seven yellow segments which make up the upper skirt (pages 37, 39, 41 & 43) and stick them together in the same way as you did for the lower skirt.

Use the Upper Skirt Gap Template (page 33) to ensure that the gap in this skirt also has the correct width before gluing the ends of the upper skirt ring together.

Step 5

Cut out the three pieces for the jig
(pages 31 & 33) and glue them together as
shown opposite.
The jig forms no part of the actual model,
but it is used in three different places to get
the right spacing between components while
the model is being made.

Step 6

Turn the jig over so the flat surface is
uppermost and the orange bits are
underneath.
Put some blutack round the rim to stop it
sliding sideways in steps 7 to 11 as the
skirts are assembled.

Step 7

Place the lower skirt centrally over the
spacing template.

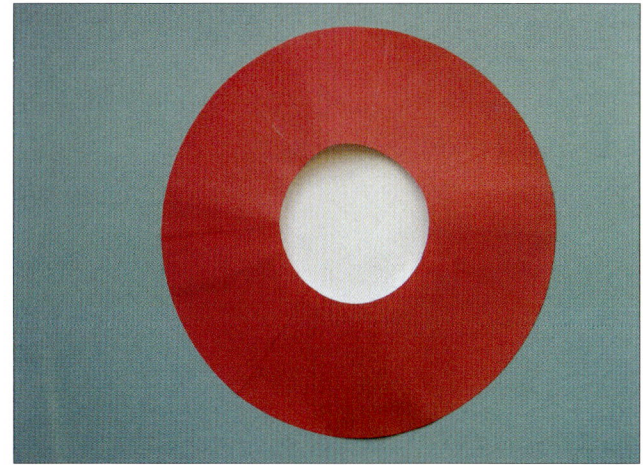

Step 8

Place the Upper skirt centrally over the
lower skirt.

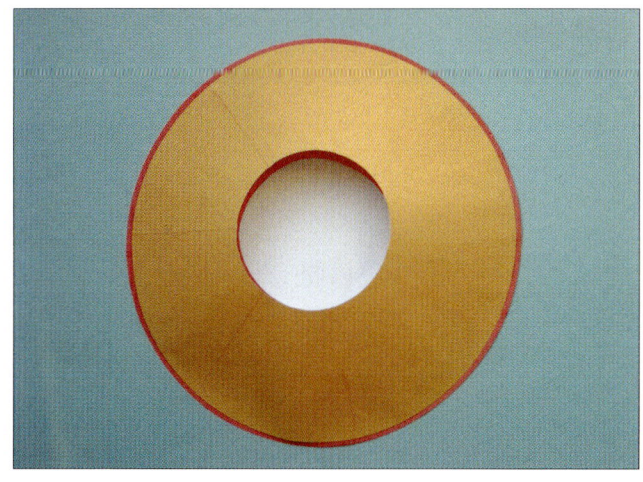

Step 9

Cut out the two pieces of the neck (pages 45 & 47). Put glue on one of the white tabs and place the red end of the other piece over the glued tab to exactly cover it. Hold a ruler along the straight edges of both pieces to make sure that the continuous straight edge is really straight. Leave for a few minutes for the glue to dry, then put glue on the remaining white tab and join the ends exactly together so no white of the tab shows.

Step 10

Gently dimple the neck into the shape shown opposite, and drop the neck into the holes in the middle of the two skirts.

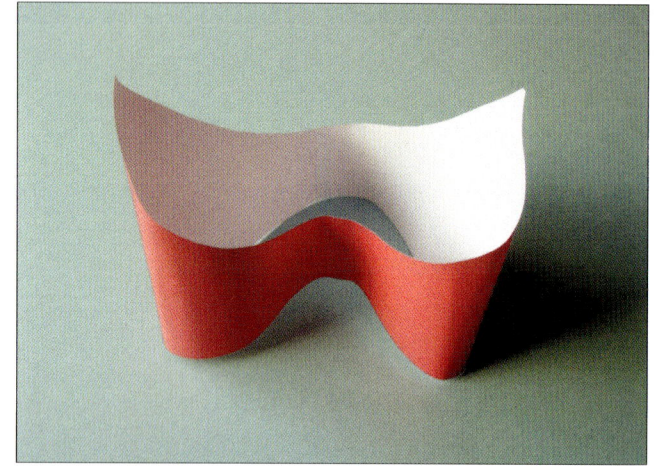

Step 11

Open the neck out so that it fits the holes in the skirts with the lower edge resting on the spacing template.

Step 12

Put glue all along the join between the upper and lower skirts.

Step 13

Put glue all along the join between the neck and the upper skirt.

Step 14

Cut out the parts for the motor tube (page 23), then bend the tube segments into shape using a ruler to make sure the bends are straight.

Step 15

After bending them into shape, glue each segment in turn into a tube.
Then bend and glue the joiner segment.
Finally put glue all over the outside of the joiner segment and insert it up to half its length in one tube and half its length into the other tube to make one long motor tube.

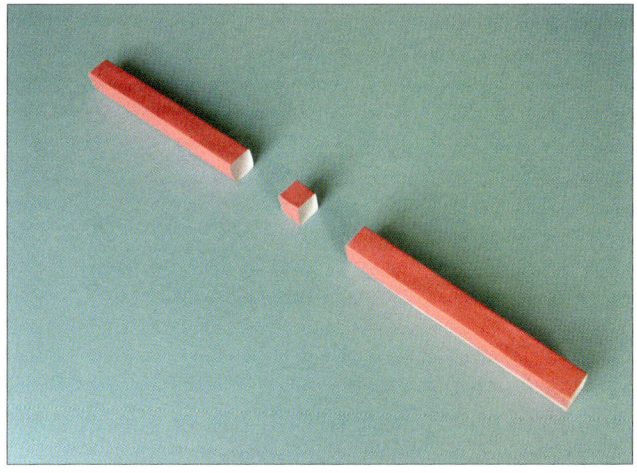

Step 16

Cut out the cylinder front end and the cylinder back end (pages 19 & 21).
For each of the cylinder ends, use a steel ruler, a sharp pointed knife, and a kitchen cutting board to cut along the black lines.
Fold the triangular tabs outwards to make a square hole in each cylinder end.
Check that the motor tube will go through each square hole, adjusting the tabs until it will.

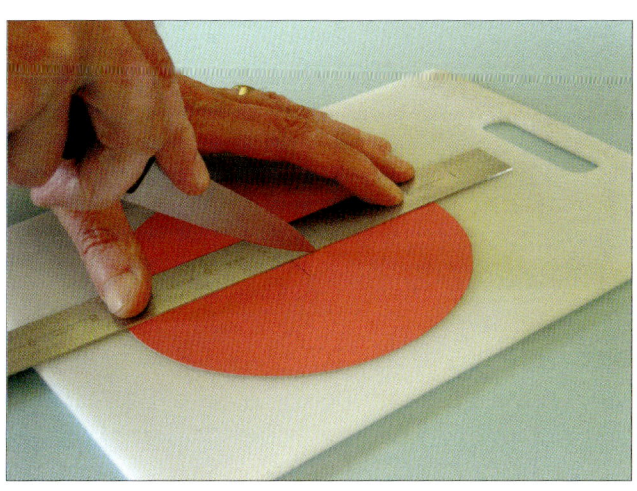

Step 17

Cut out the two halves of the cylinder (pages 49 & 51) and glue them together using their white tabs.

Make the joins as exact as possible, ensuring that the white tabs are completely covered but only just.

Leave the first join to dry for a few minutes before gluing the second join.

Step 18

Put the jig on the table with the flat side downwards, and position the cylinder on top of it.

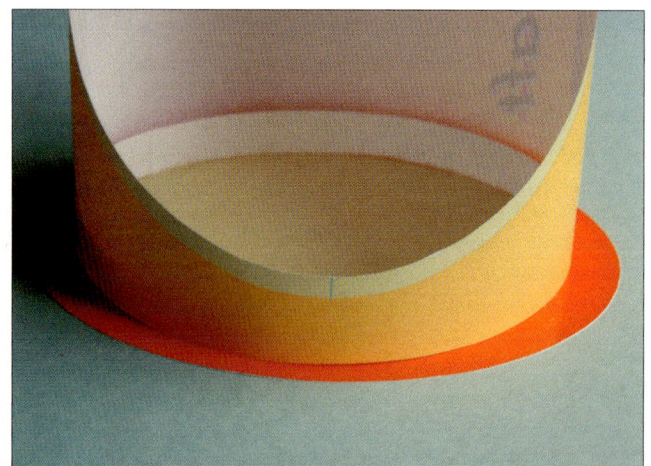

Step 19

Place the front cylinder end inside the cylinder with its red side downwards so that it rests on the jig.

Arrange it so that one of the vertical bars is lined up with the small green mark on the cylinder.

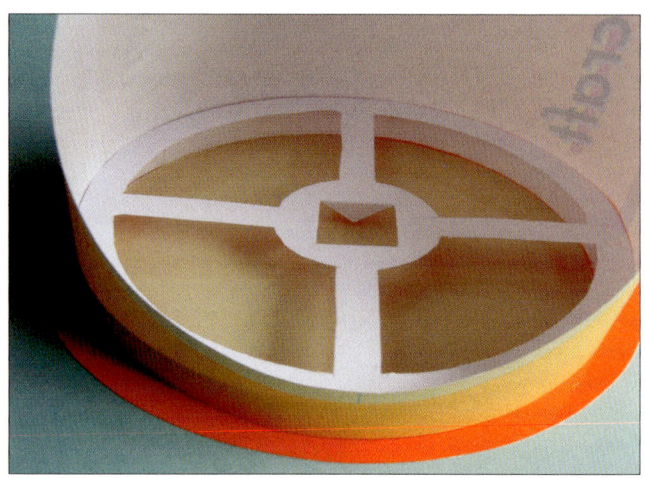

Step 20

Put glue all round the join between the cylinder and the cylinder front end.

Leave it a few minutes to dry, then, to prevent the cylinder from sticking to the jig, lift the cylinder off the jig and leave it 20 minutes or so to dry further.

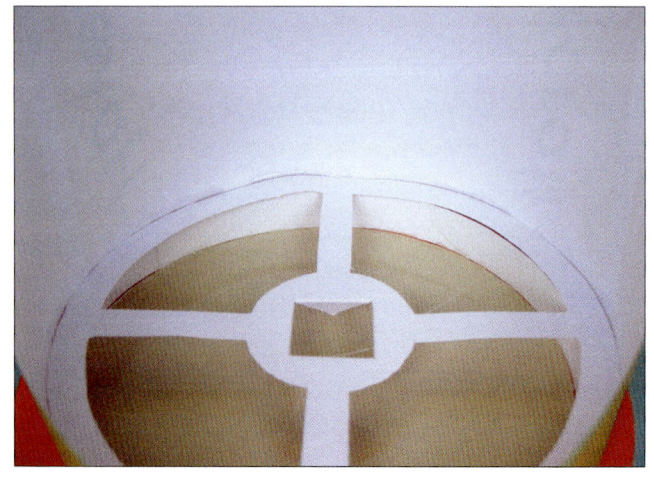

Step 21

Turn the cylinder over and stand it by its other end on the jig.
Lay the cylinder back end on the jig inside the cylinder.
Push the motor tube through the square hole in the cylinder front end and down through the square hole in the cylinder back end.
This is to line up the hole in the back end with the hole in the front end.

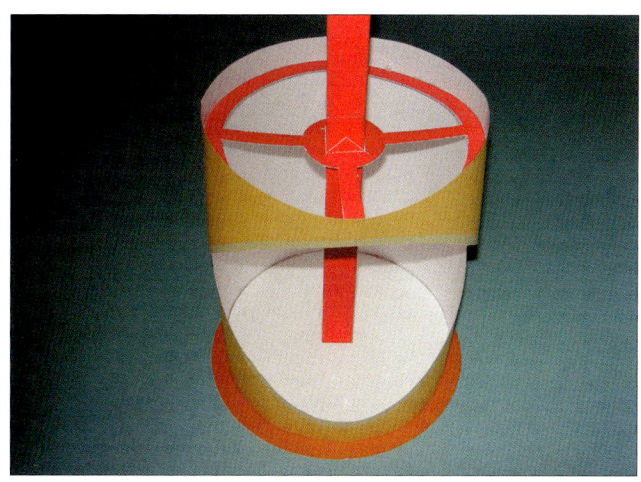

Step 22

Put glue all round the join between the cylinder and the cylinder back end.
Don't put any glue round the join between the motor tube and the cylinder back end just yet.
The motor tube is fixed in place at step 26 after the tube has been correctly positioned.

Step 23

Place the cylinder assembly on the skirt assembly.
Look carefully at the line of the join between the cylinder and the neck, and move the cylinder until the neck is positioned along the boundary of the yellow colour on the cylinder.
Put a dab of glue on each of the red pointed parts of the neck to hold the cylinder in place on the neck, then leave it to dry.

Step 24

Lift the model by the motor tube and put glue all round the join between the neck and the cylinder.
Leave to dry.

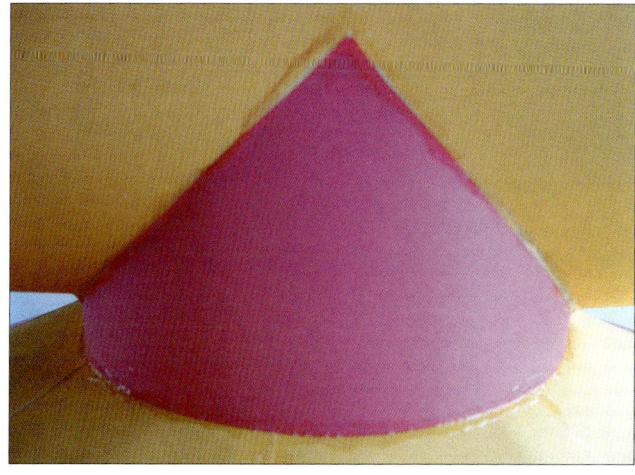

Step 25

Turn the assembly upside down and hold it by the motor tube.
Put glue all round the join between the neck and the lower skirt.
Leave to dry.

Step 26

Turn the model upright.
Carefully move the motor tube forwards through its holes in the cylinder ends until it protrudes by 3.5 cm in front of the cylinder front end.
Fix the motor tube to the cylinder by gluing the triangular tabs on each cylinder end to the motor tube. Just lift each tab up in turn, put a dab of glue underneath then press into place.

Step 27

Cut out the parts for the propeller and the fan (pages 25, 27 & 29).
Place each of the propeller halves and each of the fan halves in turn on a few sheets of scrap card and use a pair of scissors or other pointed object to make a hole at the centre the size of the white dot.

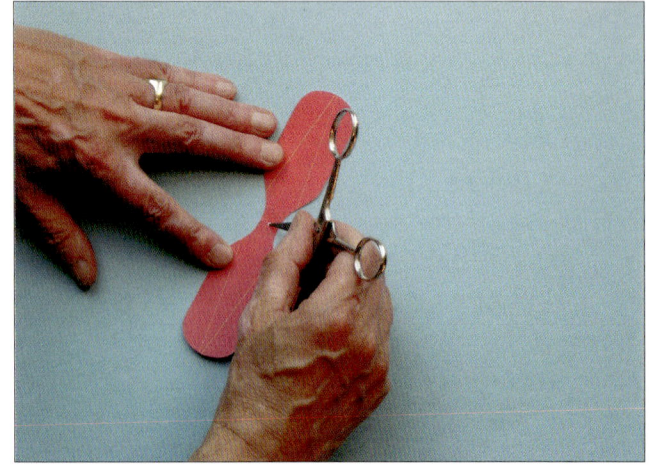

Step 28

Use the edge of a ruler to bend the propeller and fan blades along the solid yellow lines.
Bend along the solid lines downwards to 45 degrees.

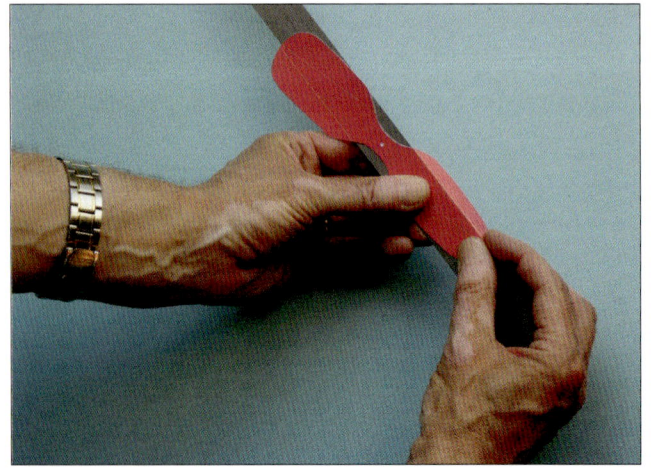

Step 29

Use the edge of a ruler to bend the propeller and fan blades along the dotted yellow lines.
Bend along the dotted lines upwards to 45 degrees.

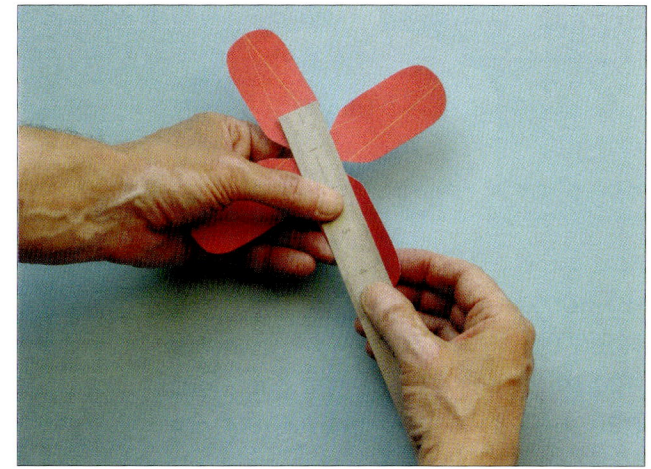

Step 30

Cut out the motor tube cap parts (page 23).
Use scissors or a similar pointed object to make a hole at the centre of each motor tube cap.
Cut along the black lines.
Bend along the yellow lines.
For each cap separate a 9mm press stud into its two halves.

Step 31

Fix a press stud into the hole of each motor cap.
Put glue on the four tabs of each cap and make up the two motor caps.

Step 32

Lay the two halves of the propeller together and put a 9mm press stud through the central hole to hold them together.
Put plenty of glue on the inside surface of each blade and glue the blades together.
The two blades are identical so it doesn't matter which one is in front and which is at the back.

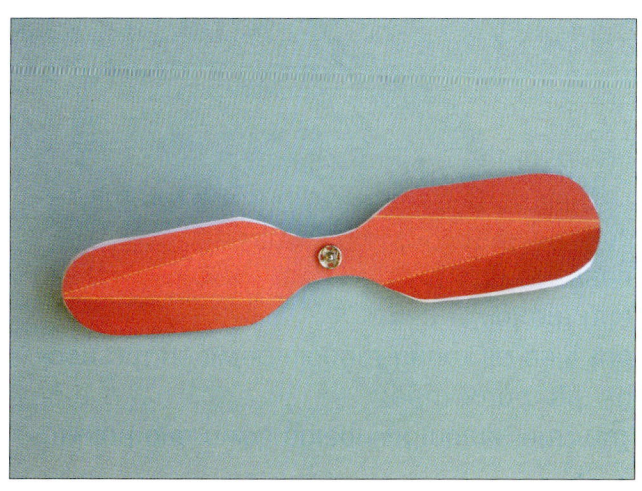

Step 33

Remove the larger half of the press stud and put the inner hub piece in place using plenty of glue.
Replace the half of the press stud on top.

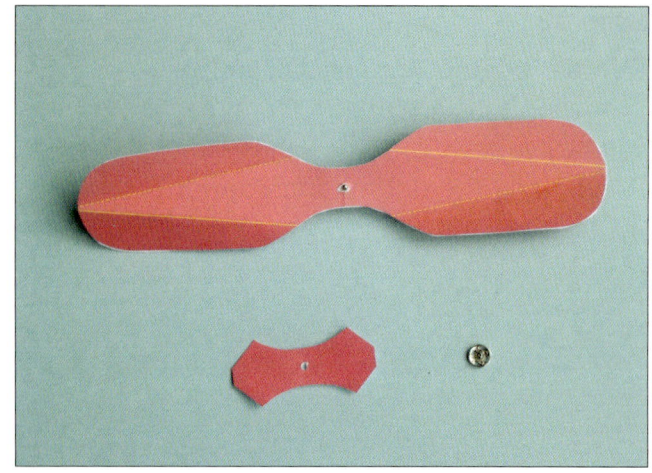

Step 34

The finished propeller should look like the picture on the right.
Follow corresponding steps to get the fan to the same stage.

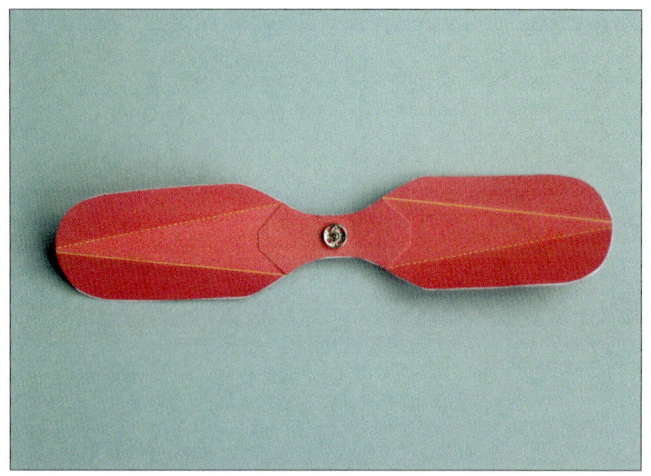

Step 35

Use long-nose pliers to straighten out a paperclip and begin bending it into shape using the pattern on page 29.

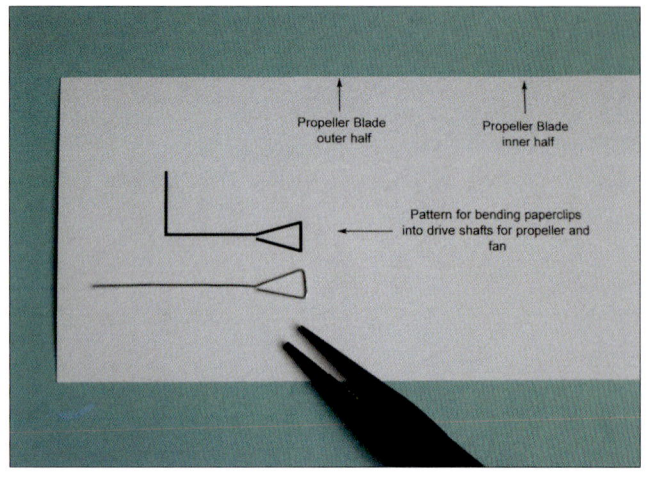

Step 36

Thread one of the nose caps and the propeller onto the shaft so that the rounded noses of the press studs meet.
Use pliers to bend the protruding end at a right angle following the pattern.

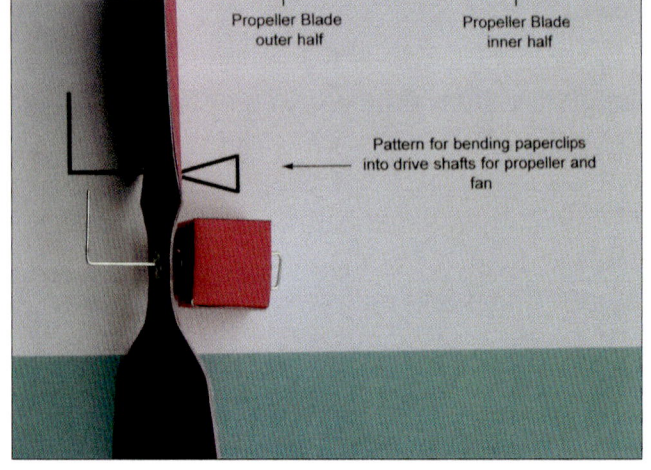

Step 37

Put plenty of glue on the propeller outer hub cap and stick it on the front of the propeller to hold the spindle firmly in place.

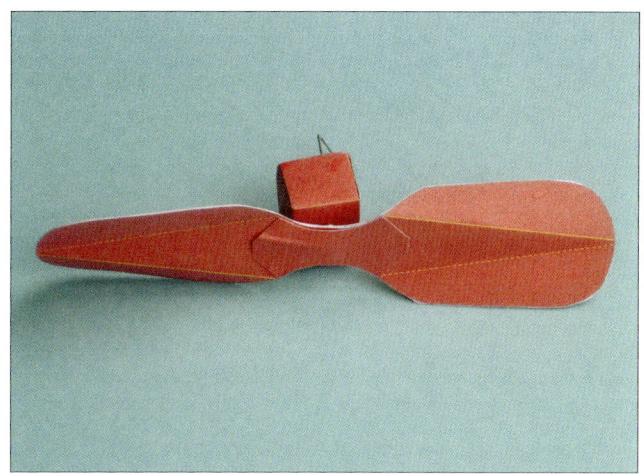

Step 38

Follow corresponding steps to complete the fan assembly.

Step 39

The fan restraint uses a spent match which is 4.5cm long.
Wrap part 2 of the fan restraint round the match, then unfurl it.
Cover the inside with glue and wrap it round the match again.
This is a bit messy!
Pull the match out before the glue sets, then put it back in again when the glue has had time to dry.

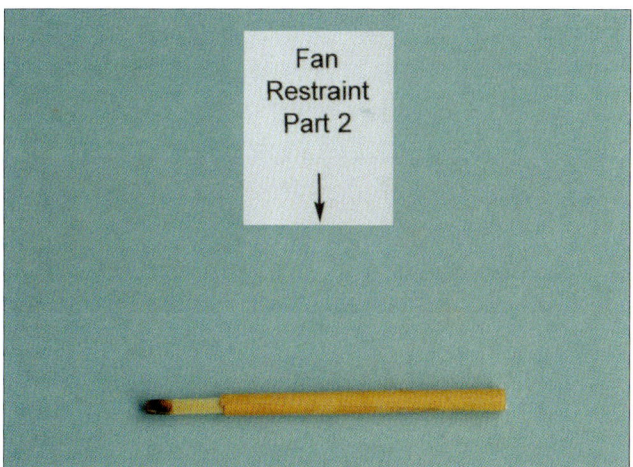

Step 40

Glue part 1 of the fan restraint to the underside of part 1.

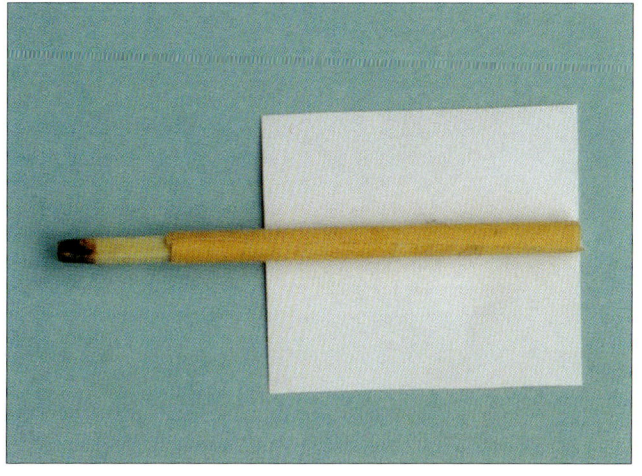

Step 41

Glue the completed fan restraint to the top of the cylinder in the middle at the front.

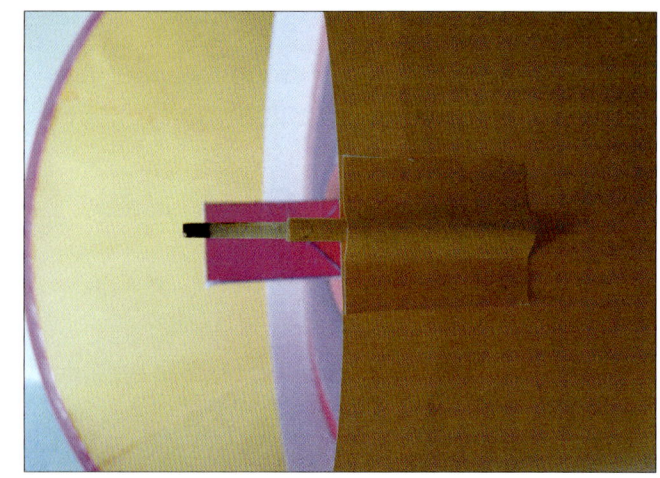

Step 42

Unbend a paperclip except one end and stick the straightened part to a pencil with cellotape.
This makes a tool with which to thread the motor through the motor tube.

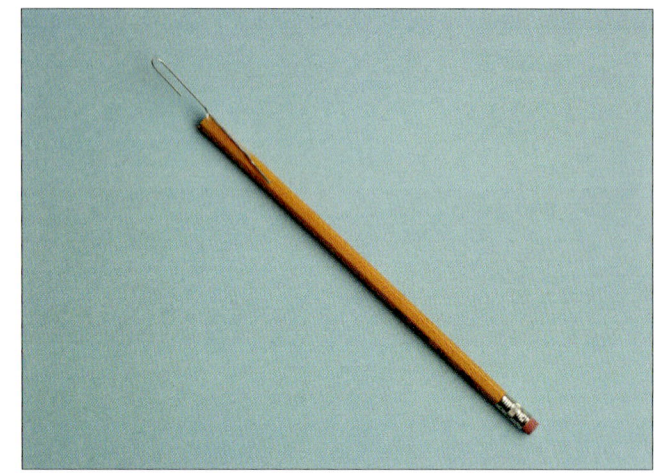

Step 43

Cut a length of model aeroplane rubber.
Cut either a 124cm length of 1/8th inch wide rubber or 64cm of 1/4 inch wide rubber.
Tie the ends together with a reef knot and trim the loose ends off.
If you used 1/8th inch rubber. make it into two loops.
If you used 1/4 inch rubber, leave it as a single loop.

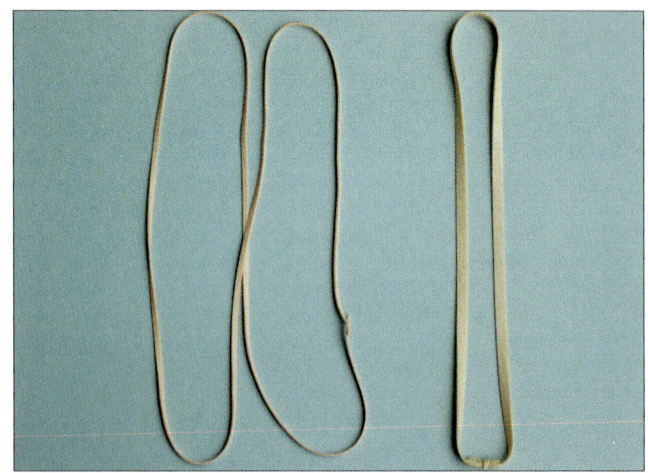

Step 44

Hook the rubber over the fan shaft at one end and over the hook on the pencil at the other end.

Step 45

Thread the rubber motor through the motor tube by lowering the pencil into the tube until it comes out at the back end.

Step 46

Let the fan assembly fit into place at the front.

Step 47

Unhook the pencil at the back end of the motor tube and hold the rubber band in place while you hook the propeller shaft onto it. Let the rubber pull the propeller assembly into place.

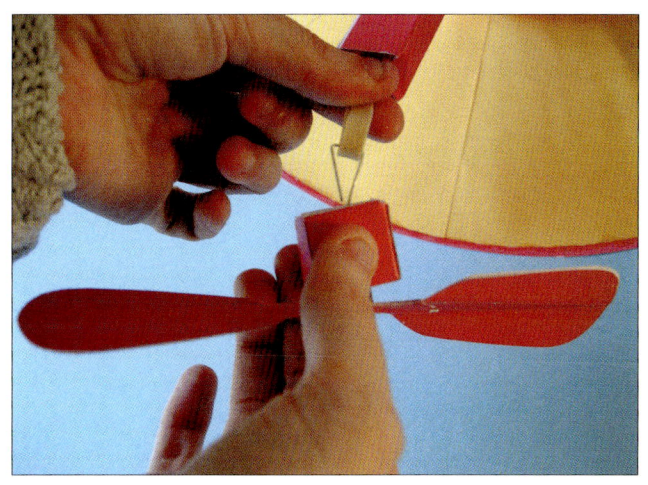

Step 48

Now we can wind the hovercraft up and let it fly!
First move the match forward until it is far enough out to stop the fan turning.
Then hold the motor tube gently with one hand, and wind up the motor by turning the propeller clockwise with the forefinger of the other hand.
Give the propeller 100 to 150 turns.

Step 49

Put the model on the floor.
Hold the propeller and motor tube with one hand.
Push the matchstick into its housing with the other hand, and release the fan.
The model should hover.
Release the propeller, and the model will fly forwards across the room.

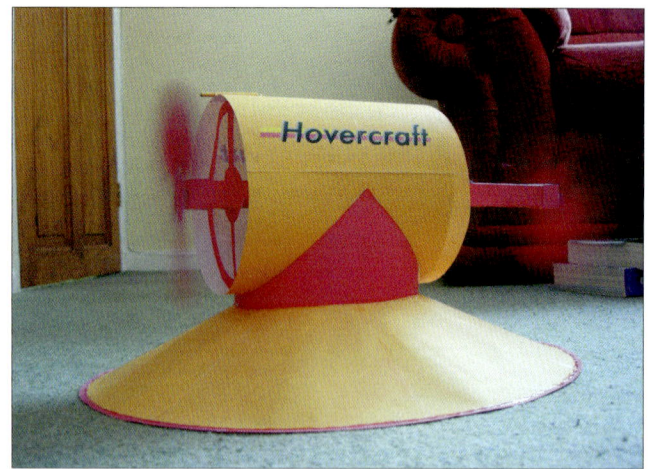

Step 50

The model will also fly across water without even getting its skirt wet!
To see this you will need to find a suitable puddle! A good place to look is a tarmac carpark immediately after a rainstorm.
Take a broom and first clear the puddle and surrounding area from small stones and any debris. Then start the model from near the puddle. It should fly over the water and land on the other side with the skirt still dry.

Step 51

Its interesting to see what happens if the propeller is fixed.
Partially straighten a paperclip and clip it to the propeller motor cap after the motor has been wound up.

Step 52

Release the fan. The model will float and move slowly forwards as the fan pulls it. This is a good way to see the model hovering. Its also interesting to see what happens if the fan is fixed. Wind the model up then release the propeller without releasing the fan. The model will not hover and will not move. This shows that hovering is essential for the model to work.

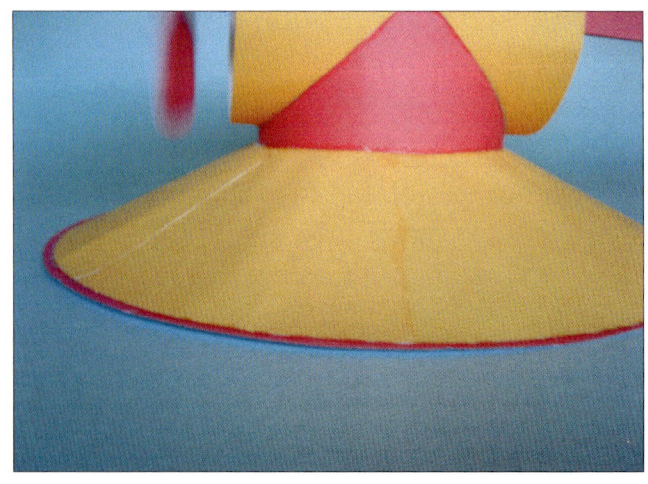

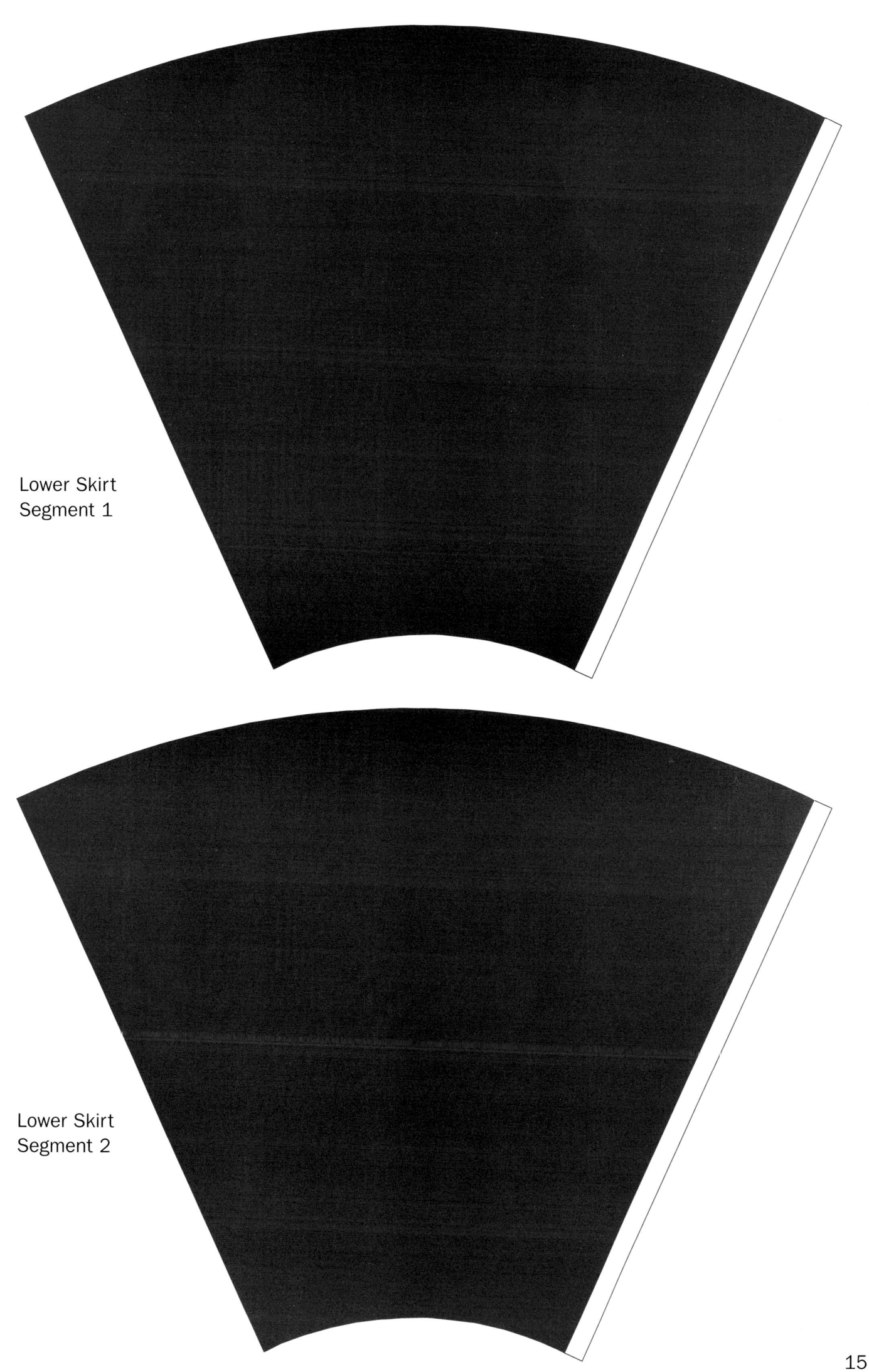

Lower Skirt
Segment 1

Lower Skirt
Segment 2

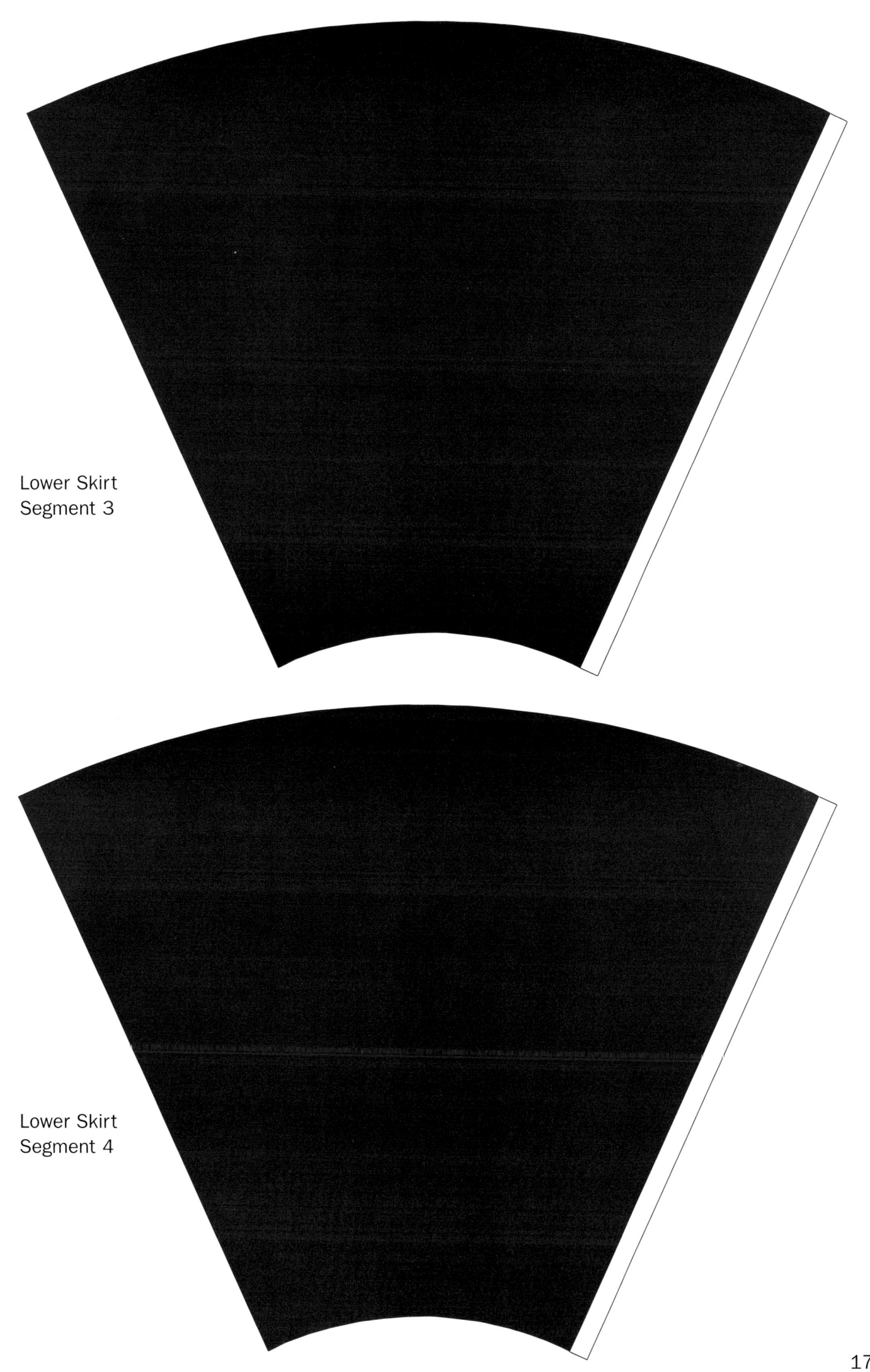

Lower Skirt
Segment 3

Lower Skirt
Segment 4

Cylinder
Front End

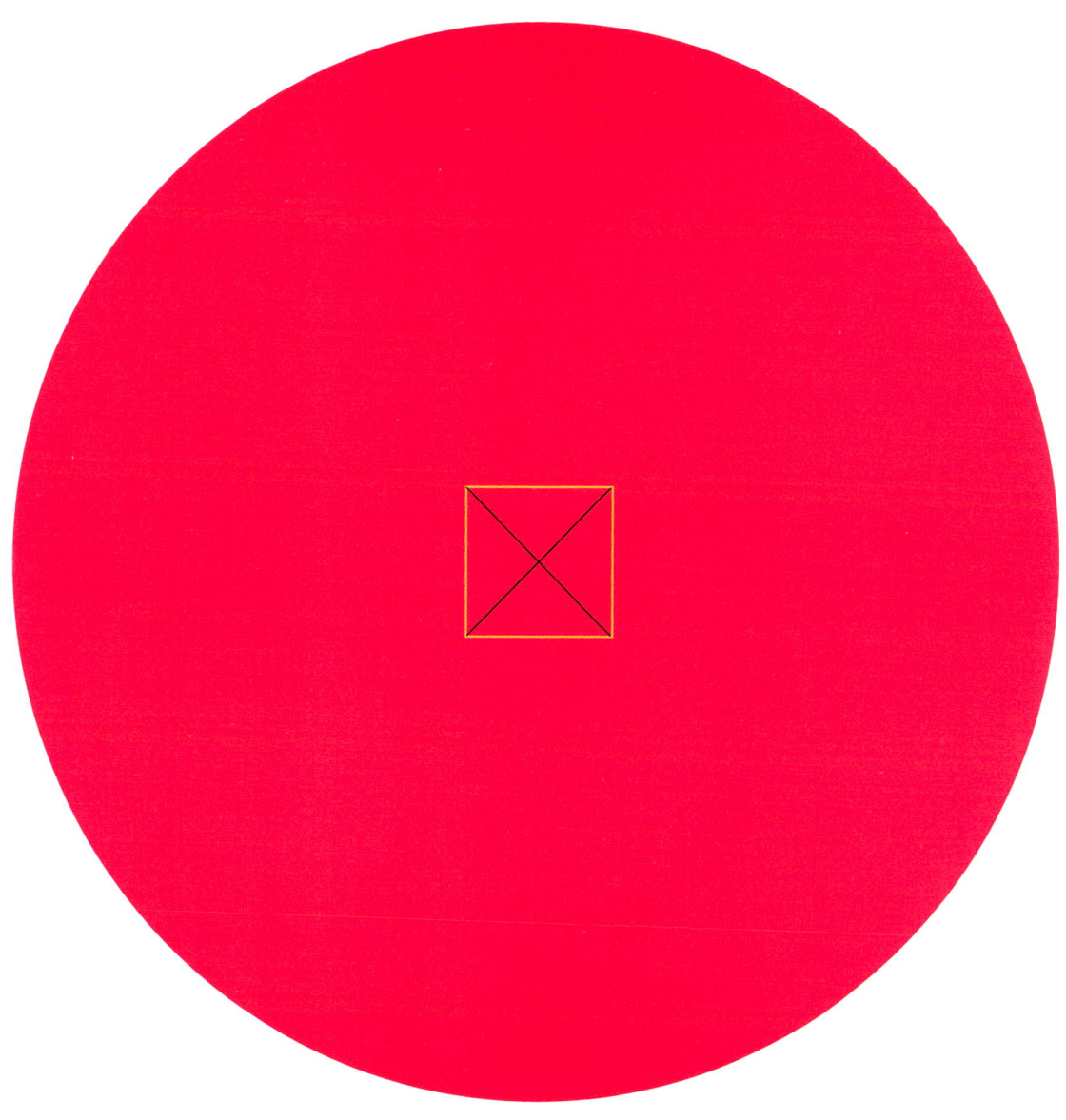

Cylinder
Back End

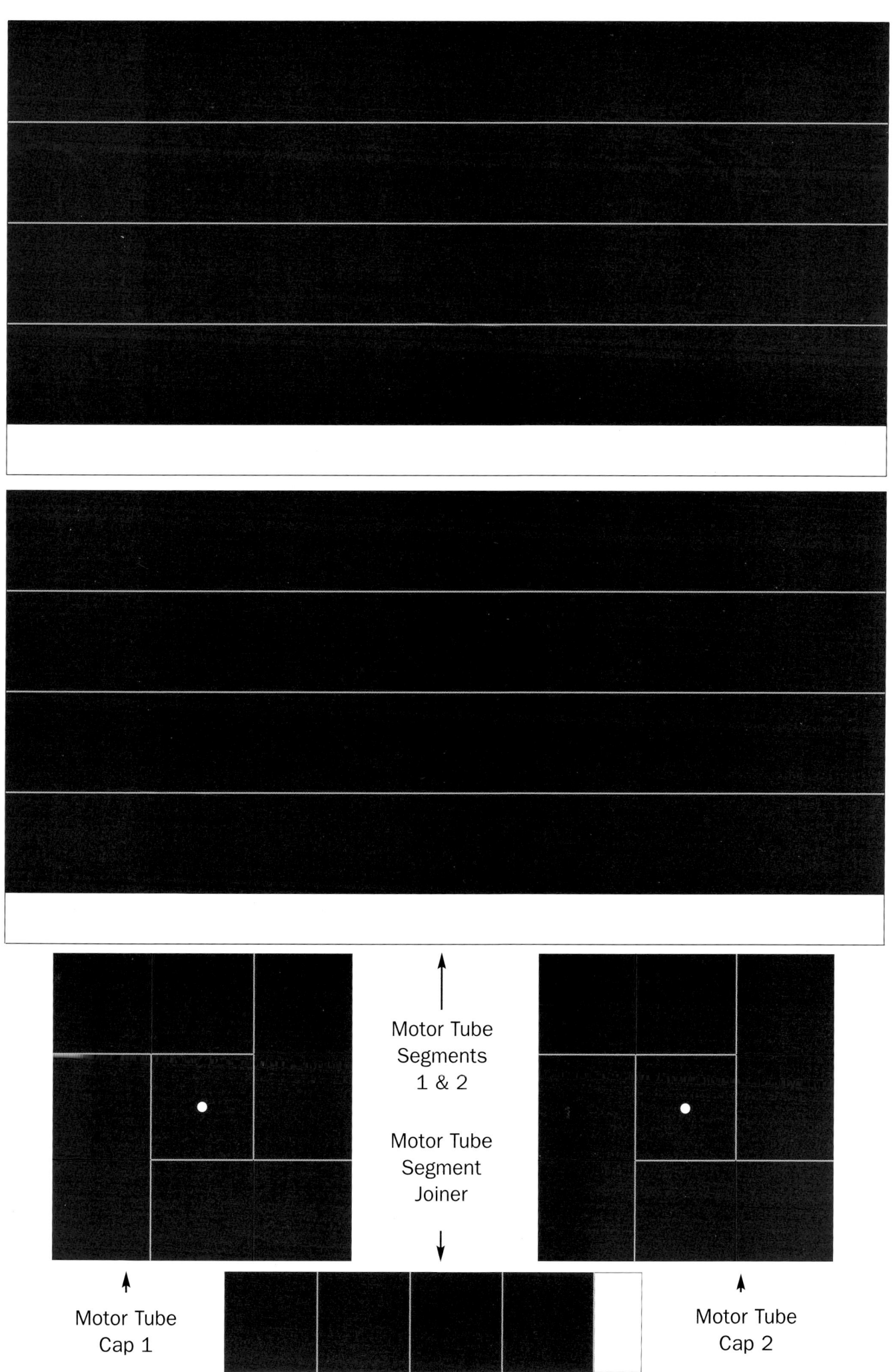

Motor Tube
Segments
1 & 2

Motor Tube
Segment
Joiner

Motor Tube
Cap 1

Motor Tube
Cap 2

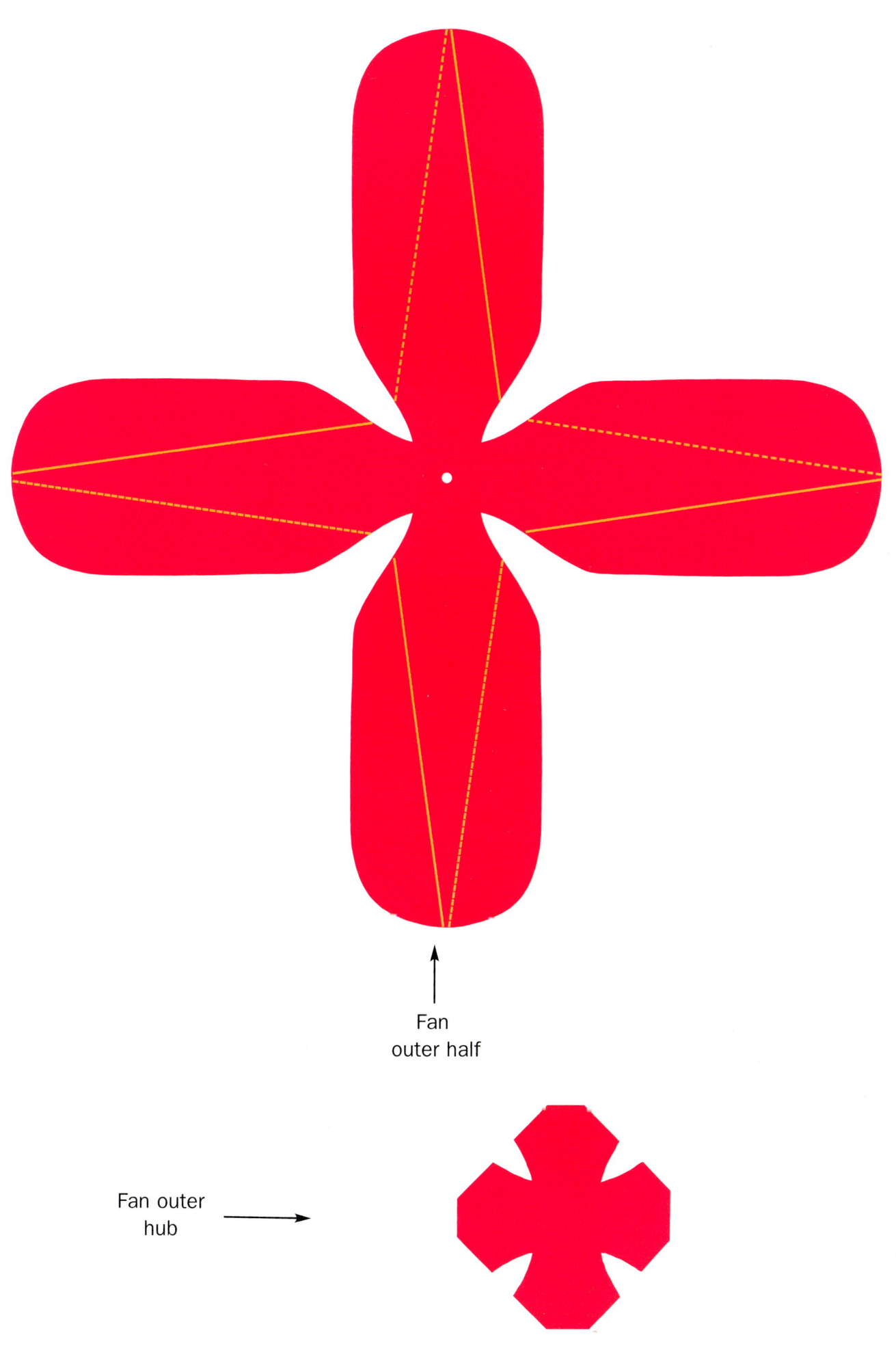

Fan
outer half

Fan outer
hub

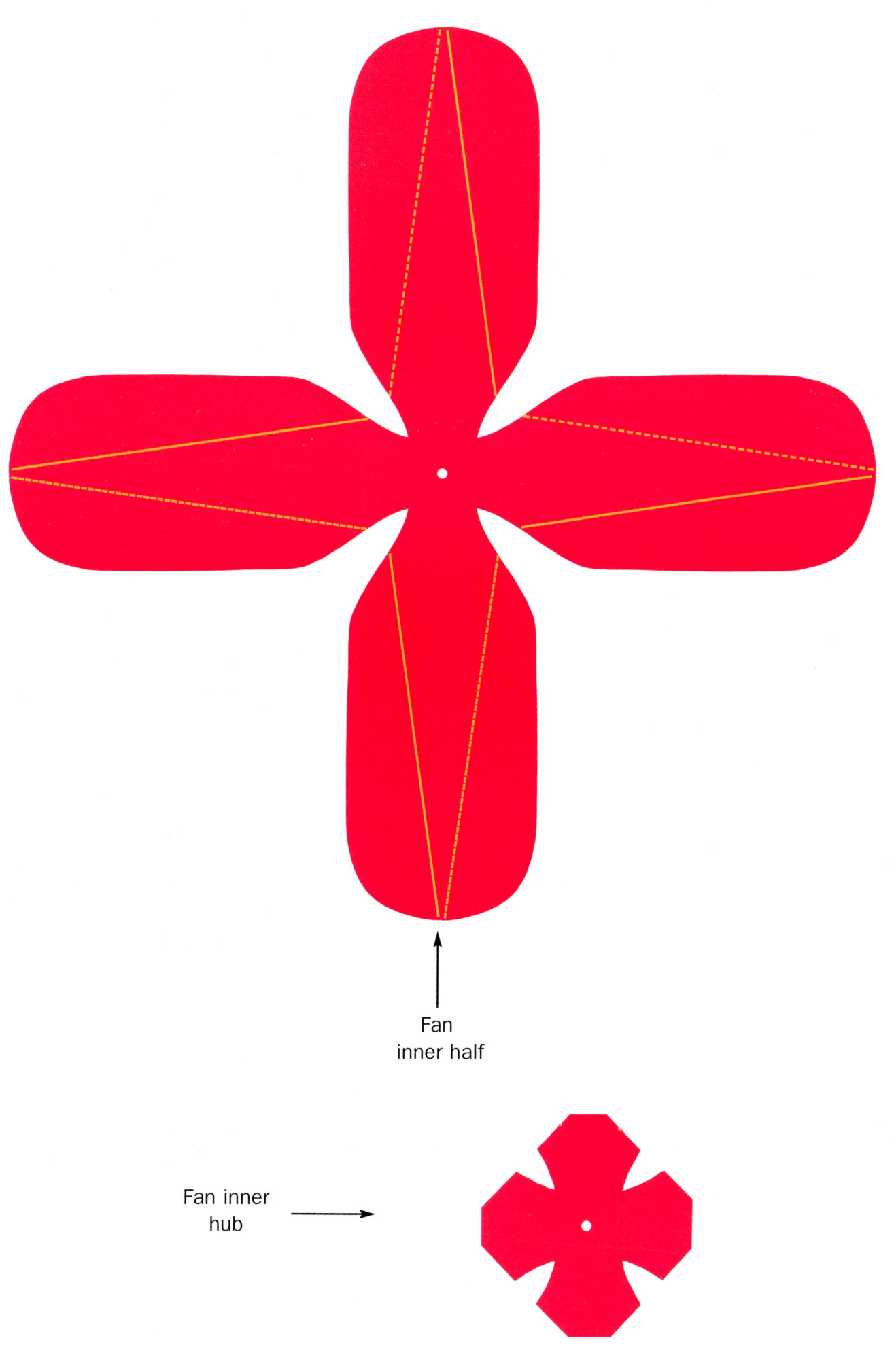

Fan
inner half

Fan inner
hub

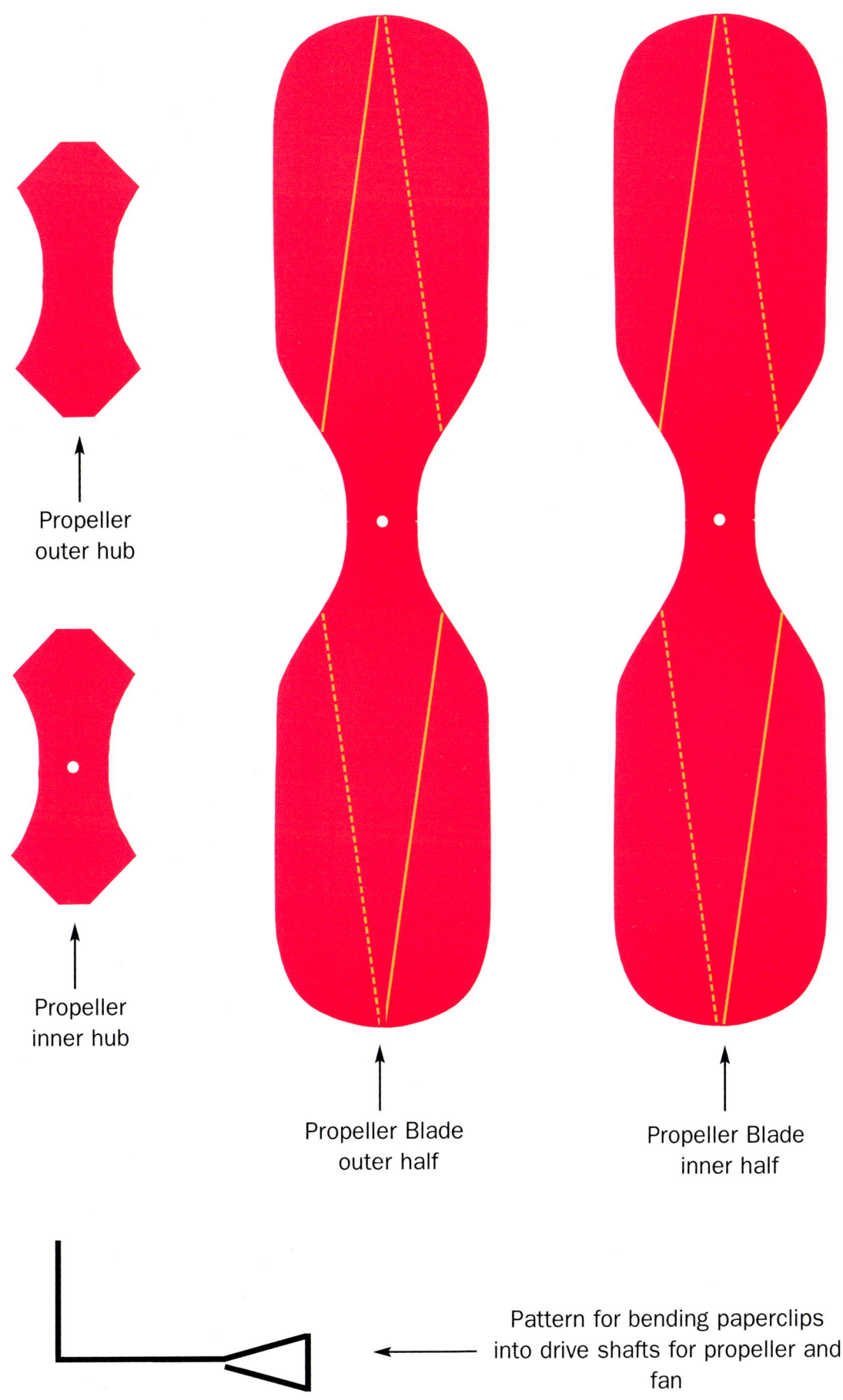

Propeller
outer hub

Propeller
inner hub

Propeller Blade
outer half

Propeller Blade
inner half

Pattern for bending paperclips
into drive shafts for propeller and
fan

Jig Base

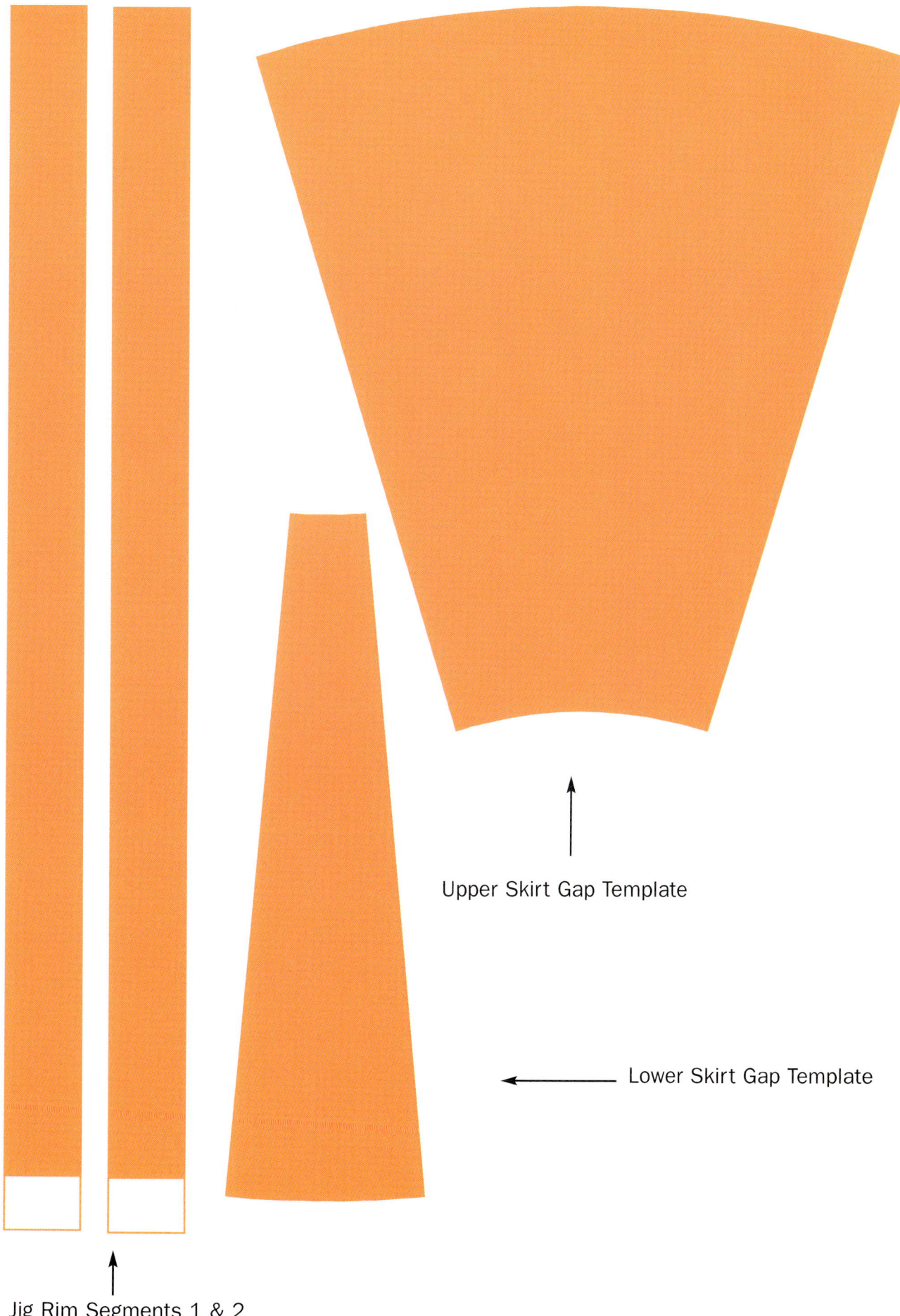

Upper Skirt Gap Template

Lower Skirt Gap Template

Jig Rim Segments 1 & 2

33

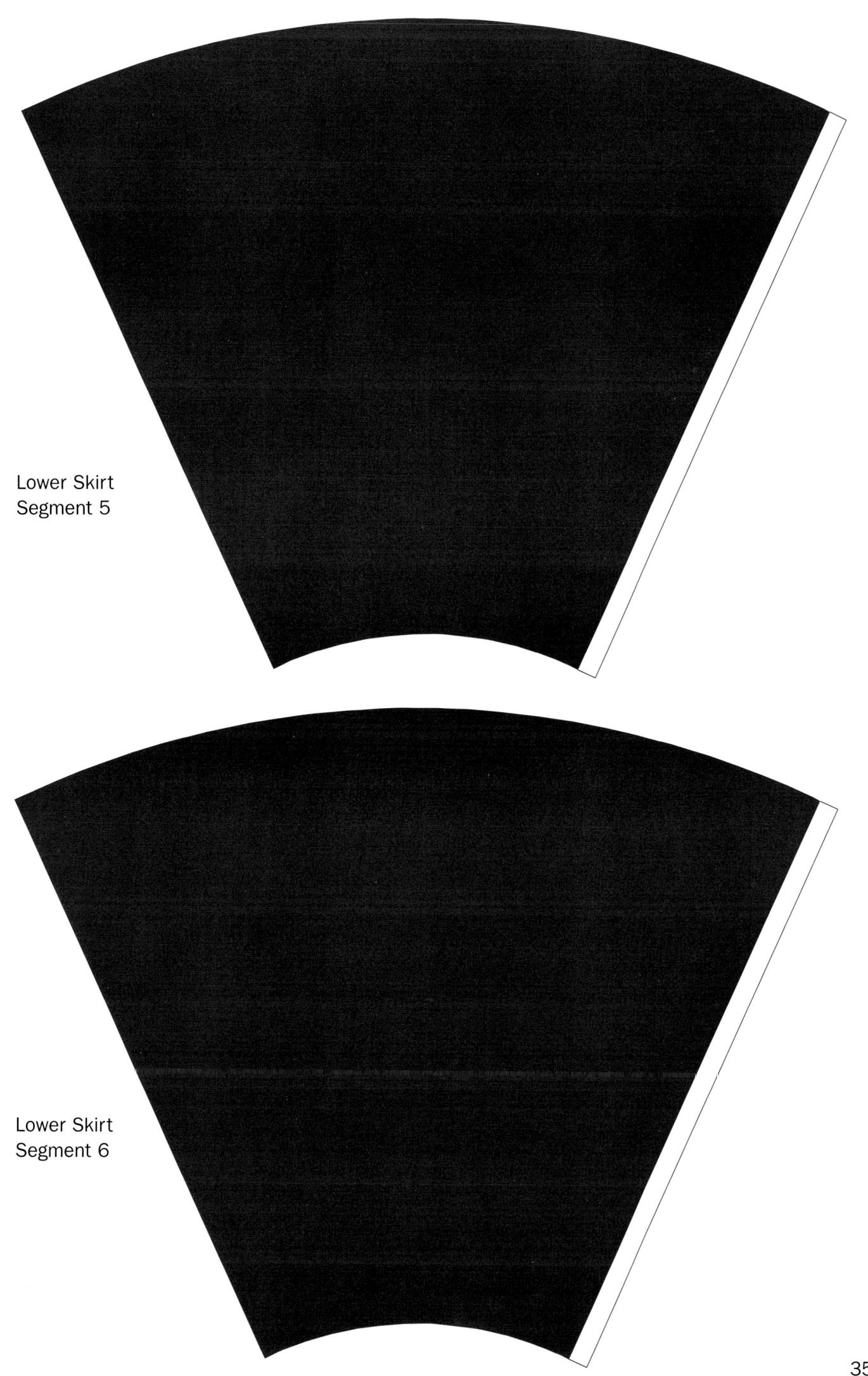

Lower Skirt
Segment 5

Lower Skirt
Segment 6

35

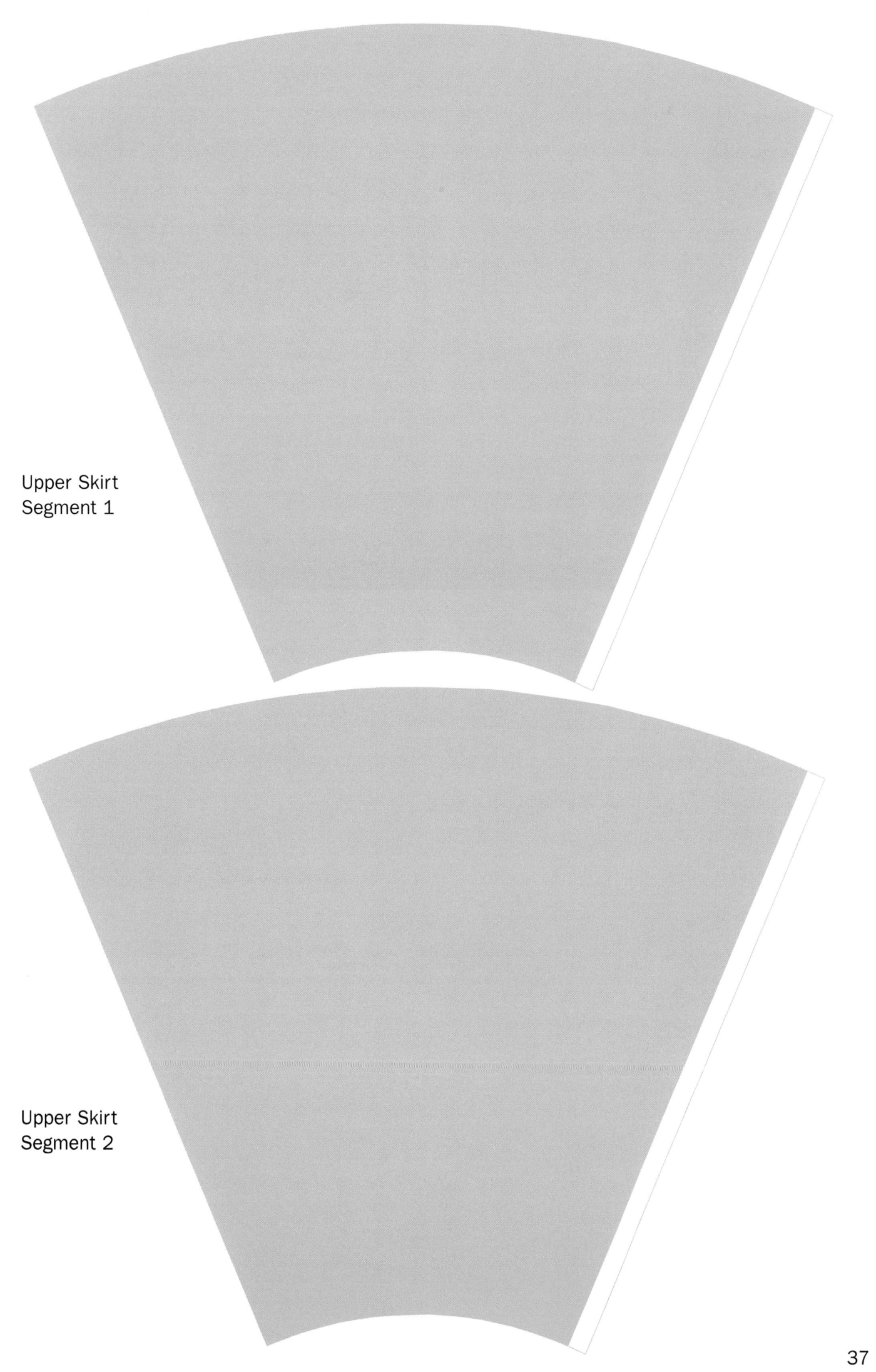

Upper Skirt
Segment 1

Upper Skirt
Segment 2

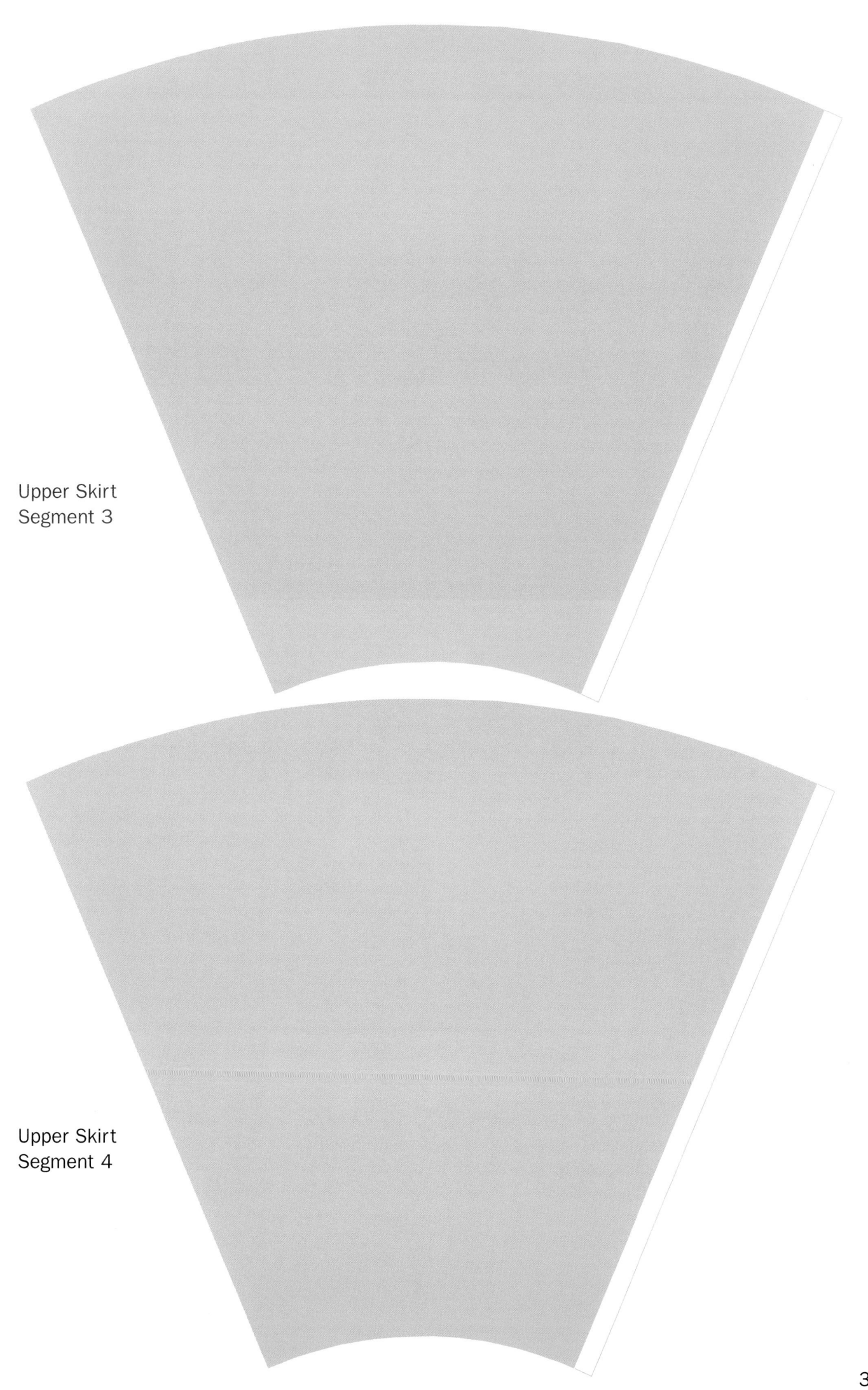

Upper Skirt
Segment 3

Upper Skirt
Segment 4

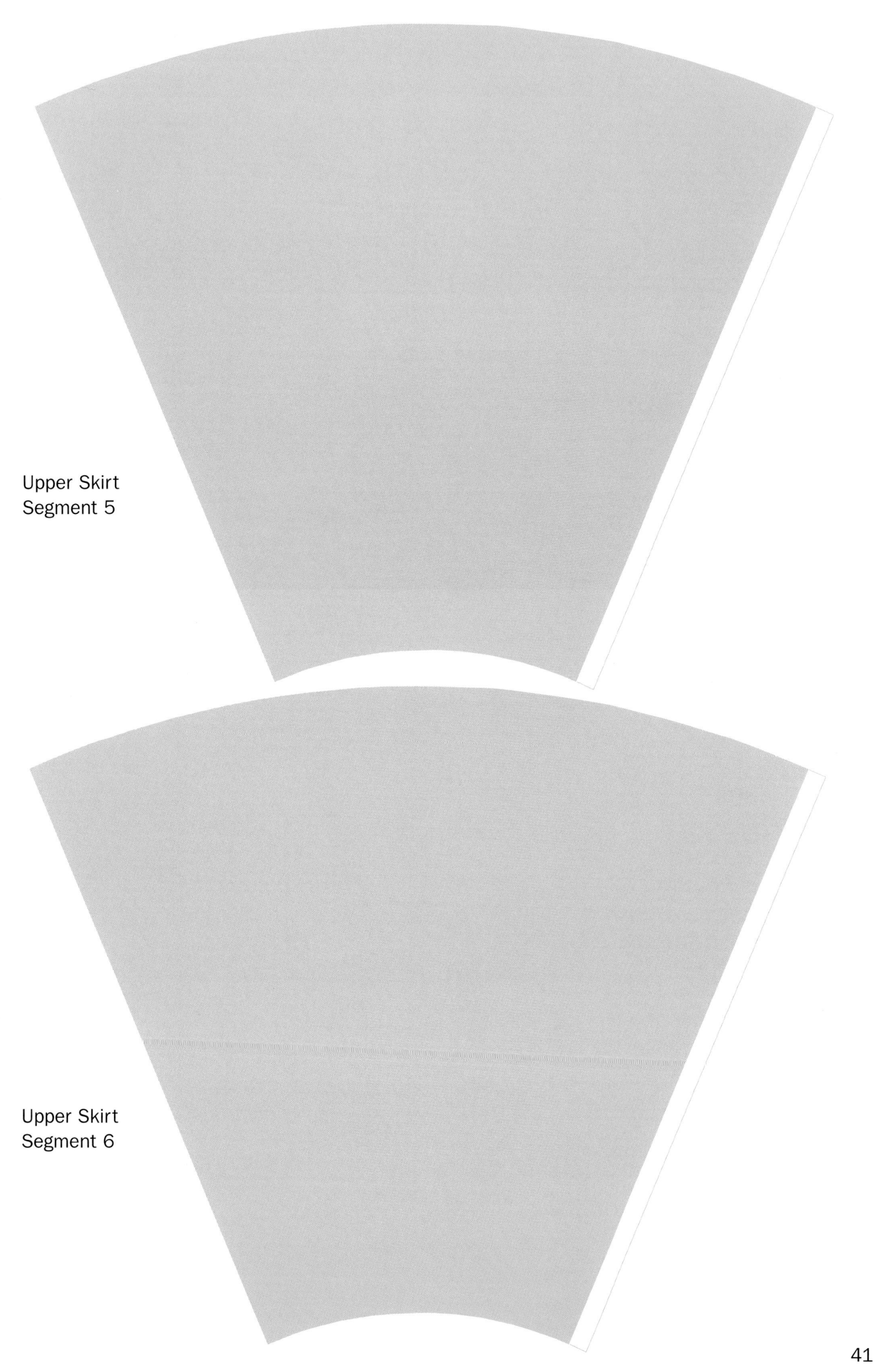

Upper Skirt
Segment 5

Upper Skirt
Segment 6

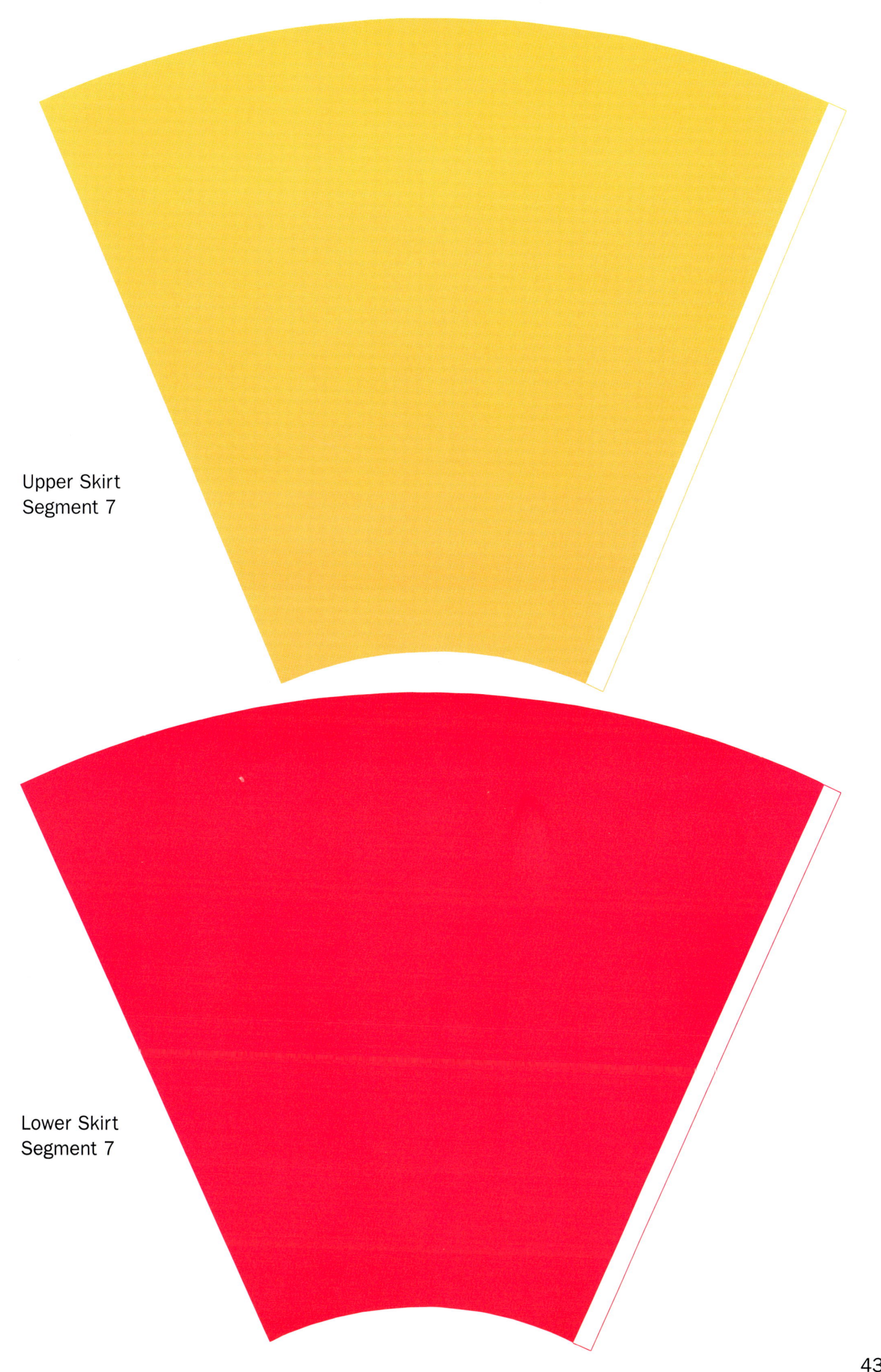

Upper Skirt
Segment 7

Lower Skirt
Segment 7

Neck
Segment 1

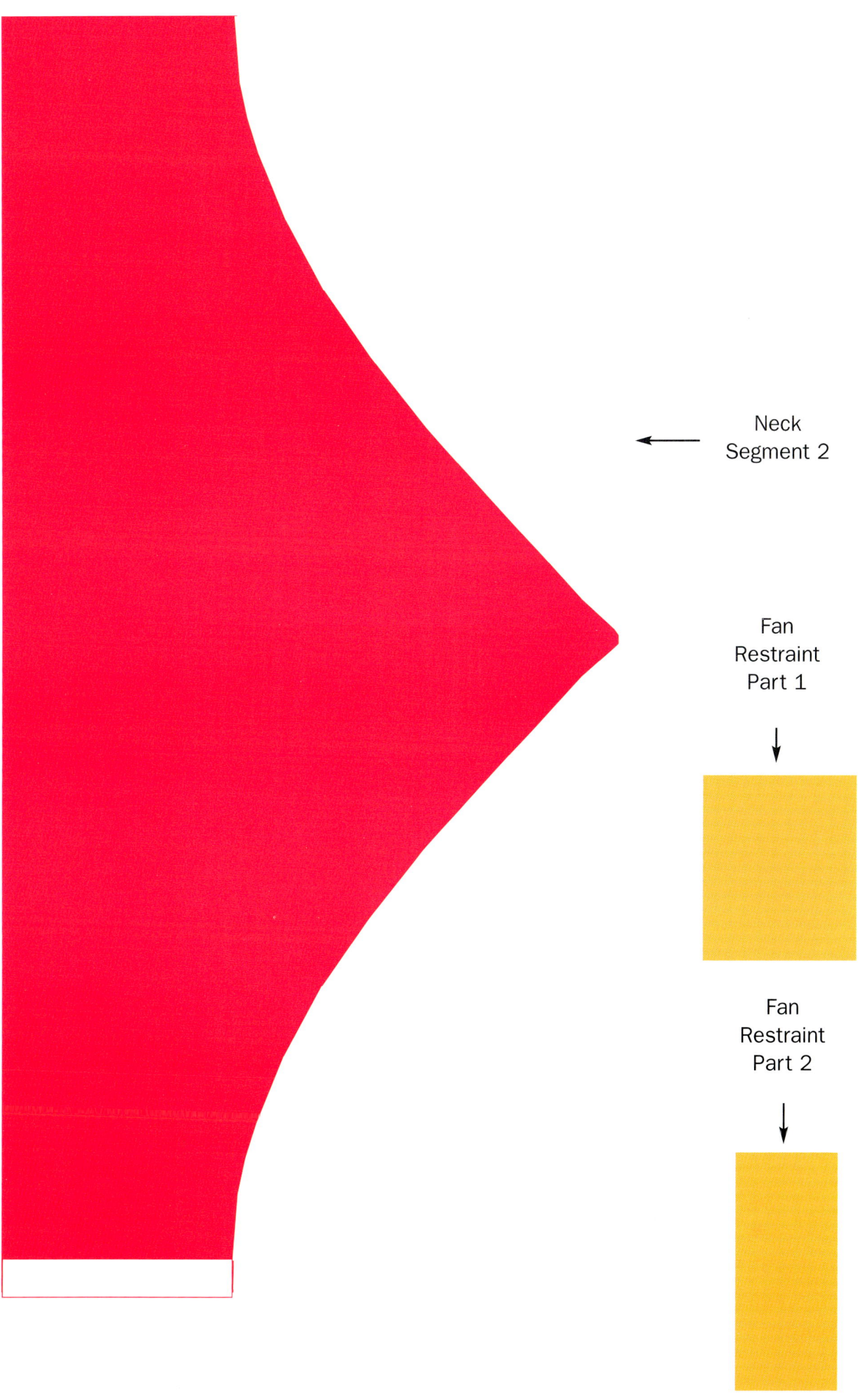

Neck
Segment 2

Fan
Restraint
Part 1

Fan
Restraint
Part 2

Hovercraft

Hovercraft